The Planets

Lesley Sims

RSVP®
RAINTREE
STECK-VAUGHN
PUBLISHERS
The Steck-Vaughn Company

Austin, Texas

D1372752

Series Editor: Pippa Pollard
Editor: Felicity Trotman
Design: Shaun Barlow
Project Manager and Electronic
    Production: Julie Klaus
Artwork: Nick Shewring
Cover Artwork: Nick Shewring
Picture Research:
    Ambreen Husain
Educational Advisor:
    Joy Richardson

Library of Congress
Cataloging-in-Publication Data
Sims, Lesley.
    The planets / Lesley Sims.
        p.   cm. — (What About)
    Includes index.
    Summary: Describes the nine planets in our solar system. Includes a discussion of topics such as gravity, the Big Bang, and the formation of the Earth.
    Hardcover   ISBN 0-8114-5506-8
    Softcover   ISBN 0-8114-4945-9
    1. Planets — Juvenile literature.
[1. Planets.]   I. Title.   II. Series.
Q8602.S56 1994
523.4—dc20   93-28660
                                CIP
                                AC

Printed and bound in the United States by Lake Book, Melrose Park, IL

3 4 5 6 7 8 9 0 LB 00 99 98 97 96

Contents

What Are Planets?

Planets are huge, spinning balls of rock or gases and liquids in space. The Earth is a planet. The word planet means "wanderer." Planets seem to wander across the sky. They are making an **orbit**, or traveling around, the sun. From the Earth, other planets look like stars. Unlike stars, they do not have their own light. They are lit up by the sun.

▽ This is how the Earth looks from space.

The Solar System

The solar system is the sun and the planets, moons, and other objects that **orbit** it. The Earth is one of nine known planets in our solar system. It is the third planet from the sun. The four planets closest to the sun are Mercury, Venus, Earth, and Mars. They are **inner planets**. Jupiter, Saturn, Uranus, Neptune, and Pluto are the five **outer planets**.

▷ The planets are different sizes. If the Earth was the size of a small ball or a cherry tomato, Mercury would be the size of a pea, and Jupiter would be as big as a pumpkin. The sun is even larger than Jupiter.

▷ The planets that orbit the sun. The inner planets have much smaller orbits than the outer planets.

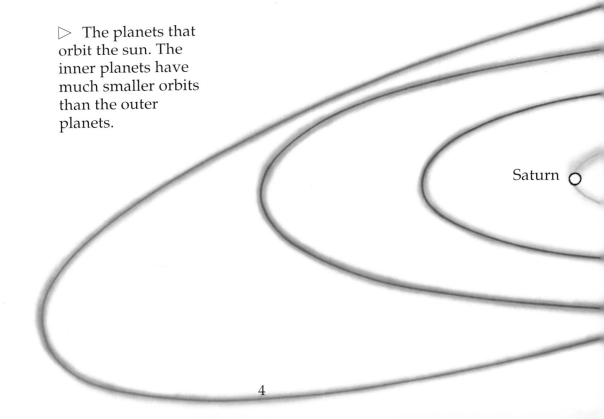

Saturn ○

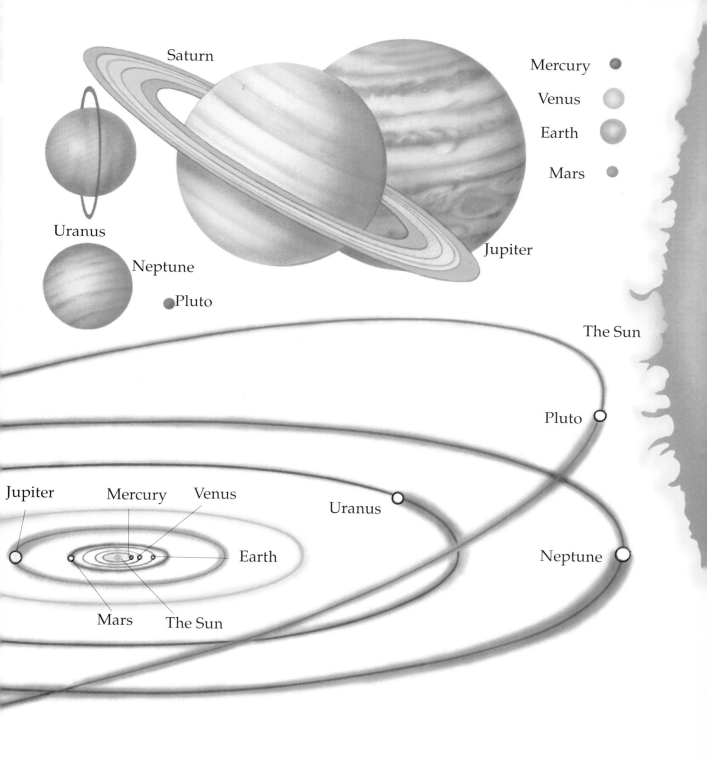

Saturn

Mercury

Venus

Earth

Mars

Uranus

Neptune

Pluto

Jupiter

The Sun

Pluto

Jupiter   Mercury   Venus

Uranus

Earth

Neptune

Mars   The Sun

Gravity

Planets are held in their orbits around the sun because of **gravity**. Gravity is an invisible force that pulls objects together. Objects with a larger **mass** have a much stronger force. The sun's gravity pulls on the planets. The force of gravity keeps us on the Earth. Gravity holds **moons** in orbit around planets. Something in orbit is called a **satellite**.

▷ The moon is a satellite of the Earth.

▽ People are lighter on the moon than on the Earth. The moon has less gravity than Earth because it has less mass.

△ The moon is
held in orbit around
the Earth by the
force of gravity.

The Big Bang

Most scientists believe that about 15 billion years ago, everything was pressed together in one lump. Suddenly the lump exploded into millions of pieces. The explosion was so fierce, it threw the pieces far out into space. This was the beginning of the universe. It is called the big bang. Millions of years later, one piece became our solar system.

▽ Everything in the universe, including this galaxy, formed as a result of the big bang. A galaxy is a large group of stars held together by gravity.

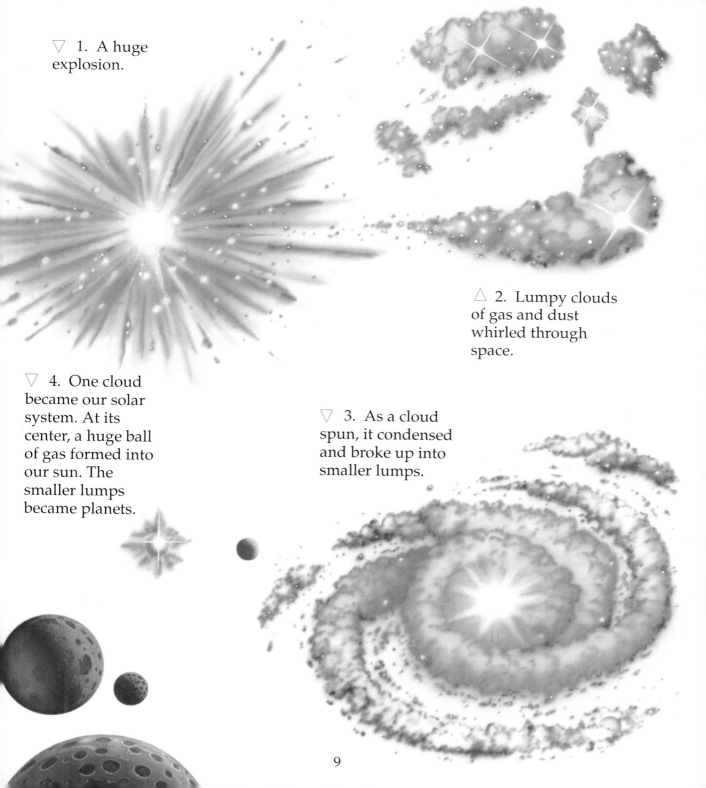

▽ 1. A huge explosion.

△ 2. Lumpy clouds of gas and dust whirled through space.

▽ 4. One cloud became our solar system. At its center, a huge ball of gas formed into our sun. The smaller lumps became planets.

▽ 3. As a cloud spun, it condensed and broke up into smaller lumps.

9

How the Earth Was Formed

The Earth began as a ball of hot, liquid rock and gases about 4.6 billion years ago. Over millions of years it cooled down. The surface hardened into a solid crust. The gases cooled into rain, which flooded the Earth and became oceans. Earth's gravity held on to an invisible layer of gases that became air. This is the **atmosphere**.

▷ Oceans cover almost three-quarters of the Earth's surface.

▽ For its first few million years, the Earth was a very hot and violent place.

▷ The Earth is made up of layers. On the outside is the hard crust. Underneath is a layer called the mantle. In the center is the core. Scientists believe that the core is liquid on the outside and solid in the middle.

Atmosphere

Crust

Mantle

Solid core

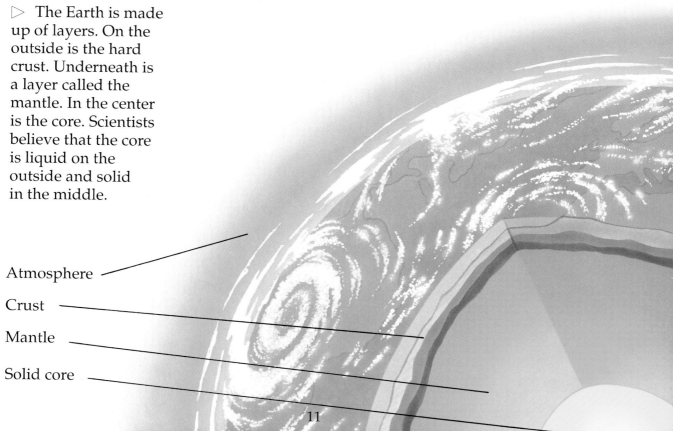

Geology

Geology is the study of the Earth. The Earth's crust is made up of separate pieces called plates. If the rock at the edges of the plates moves, earthquakes occur. Volcanoes erupt when hot, liquid rock is forced through a weak part of the Earth's crust. Mountains form when the plates push against each other.

▷ A volcano can lie quiet or inactive for years before suddenly erupting.

▽ An earthquake sends shudders through the ground, causing giant cracks in the Earth.

▽ Wind and rain
wear away the
Earth's surface. This
is called erosion.

A Year on the Earth

It takes the Earth a year to travel all the way around the sun. The Earth tilts on its **axis**. At any one time, part of the Earth is tilted toward the sun and is warmer. The part which is tilted away is cooler. As the Earth orbits the sun, this cooler part becomes the part tilting toward the sun and grows warm. These changes in temperature cause the seasons.

▷ The area around the equator faces the sun more directly than anywhere else on the Earth, so places on or near the equator are always hot.

▽ The equator is an imaginary line which runs around the Earth at an equal distance from the two poles.

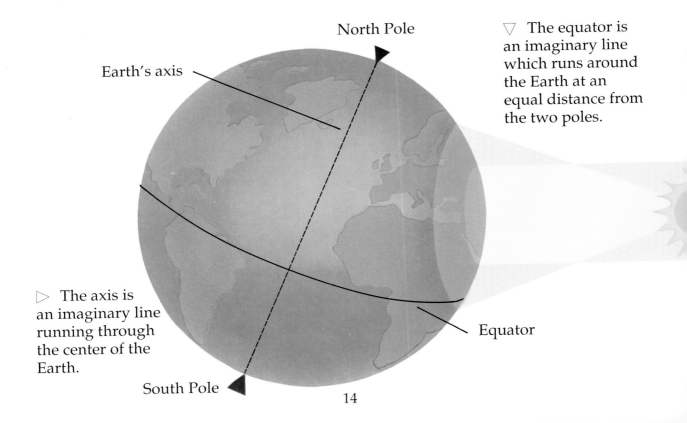

North Pole

Earth's axis

▷ The axis is an imaginary line running through the center of the Earth.

Equator

South Pole

14

▷ When the northern part of the world has winter, it is summer in the southern part of the world.

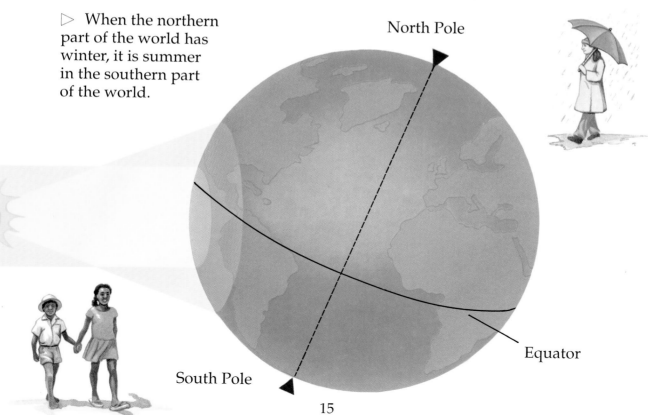

North Pole

South Pole

Equator

15

Mercury

Mercury is the nearest planet to the sun. A year on Mercury is only 88 days long. Mercury is almost three times closer to the sun than the Earth. On Mercury, it is much hotter in the daytime. The sun appears much larger there than from the Earth. It is a dry planet, covered in holes or **craters**. Scientists think these were made by rocks crashing into Mercury when it formed.

▷ This spacecraft is Mariner 10. It sent back detailed photographs of Mercury to the Earth in 1974.

▽ The surface of Mercury taken by Mariner 10.

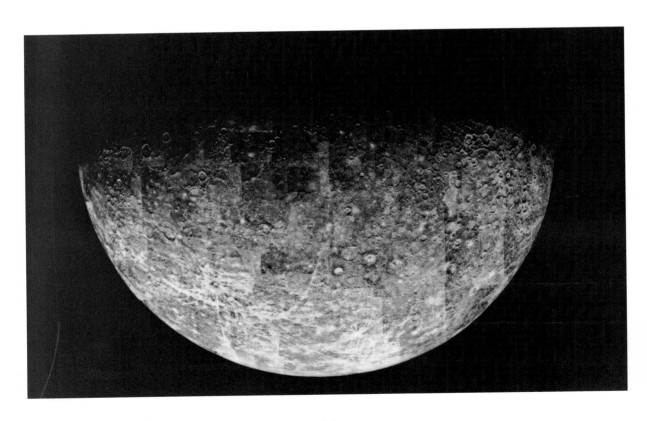

Venus

Venus is the planet closest to the Earth and only a little smaller. The surface of the planet is covered in a thick layer of clouds made of poisonous gases. These clouds reflect sunlight, so from the Earth Venus seems to shine more brightly than many stars. Beneath the clouds, Venus is rocky, dry, and very hot. The surface is hot enough to cook on.

▽ The United States and Soviet Union have sent robot spacecraft, called probes, to visit Venus. This photo of the surface of Venus was taken by a Soviet probe.

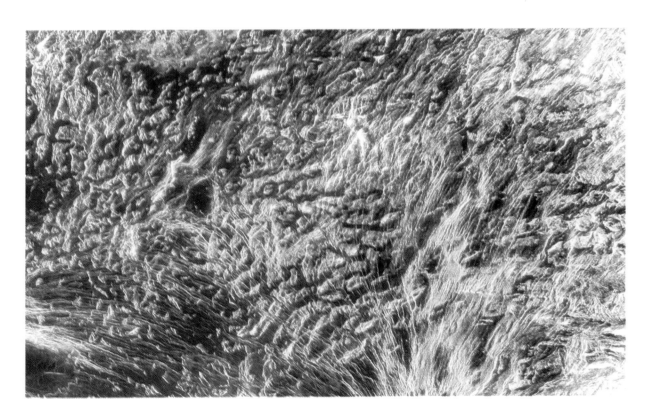

◁ Scientists believe the gas clouds that surround Venus trap the heat from the sun.

▷ This image shows what the surface of Venus is like underneath all the clouds.

yellow and green: high areas

blue: low areas

Mars

Mars is known as the Red Planet. Rusty iron dust in the rocks colors the surface a reddish-brown and turns the sky orange. Mars is a desert but a very cold one. Dry channels run over the planet, but Mars has no water on its surface. At the top and bottom of the planet are two white patches. Scientists think the water has frozen here.

▷ The surface of Mars, photographed by the American probe Viking 1, which landed on Mars in 1976.

▽ Mars has two moons, shaped like enormous potatoes. They are so small that they could both fit into one of the larger craters on our moon.

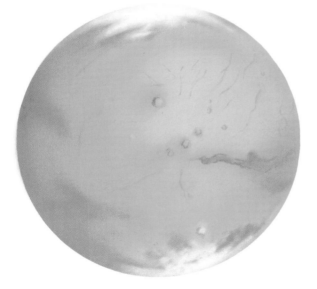

△ The ice patches at the poles of Mars may be more than one half of a mile (1km) thick.

Jupiter, the Gas Giant

Jupiter is made up of gases and liquids, although it may have a small, solid core. Jupiter measures almost 89,000 miles (143,000km) across. It has more mass than all the other planets together. Jupiter has at least sixteen moons. One of them, Ganymede, is bigger than Mercury. Jupiter has a ring made of dust, but it cannot be seen from the Earth.

▷ The Great Red Spot is in the clouds which cover Jupiter. Scientists think it is a hurricane-like storm, which has been raging for hundreds of years.

▷ This shows Jupiter with its four largest moons — Io, Europa, Ganymede, and Callisto.

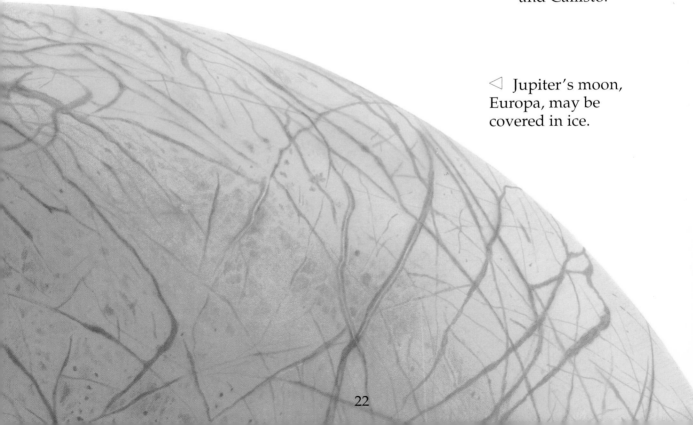

◁ Jupiter's moon, Europa, may be covered in ice.

Saturn

Saturn is the second largest planet in the solar system. It is another gas giant, with eighteen moons. Saturn is surrounded by the most beautiful rings. They are made of chunks of rock and ice, some as small as dust and others as big as a house. Even though Saturn is so big, it is very light. Saturn could float, if there were a swimming pool large enough!

▽ Although Saturn's rings are wide, they are very thin. Sometimes we can hardly see them from the Earth.

◁ Mimas is one of Saturn's many moons. It has a crater that covers almost a third of its diameter. If the rock that caused it had been any bigger, Mimas would have been smashed to pieces.

△ Saturn has over 1,000 rings.

25

Uranus, Neptune, and Pluto

These planets were discovered with the help of telescopes. Uranus is hidden by a blue-green cloud of gas. It spins on its side. Uranus takes about 84 Earth years to orbit the sun. A year on Neptune lasts over 164 Earth years. Because Neptune is so far from the sun, it is very cold and dark. Pluto is smaller than our moon. It has a tiny moon of its own.

▷ Triton is a large satellite of Neptune. It has eruptions that spurt out gas and dust. Frozen gas gives Triton a pink glow.

▽ Miranda is one of Uranus's fifteen satellites. It seems to be made up of lots of pieces, like a jigsaw puzzle. It may have broken up thousands of years ago and put itself back together in the wrong order.

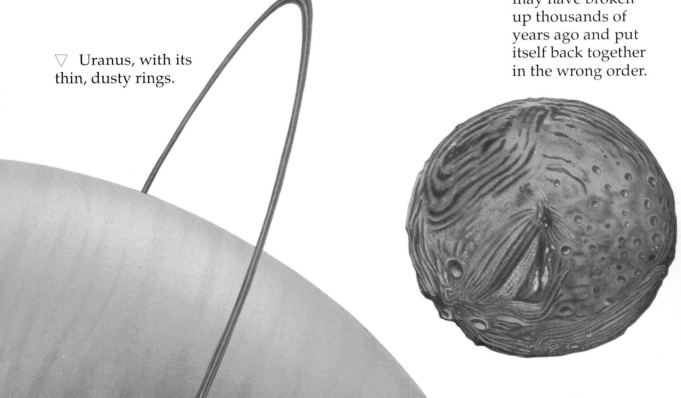

▽ Uranus, with its thin, dusty rings.

Asteroids, Meteors, Comets

Asteroids are chunks of rock and metal. They are found in the Asteroid Belt between the inner and outer planets. Other bits of rock and metal sometimes break through the Earth's atmosphere and burn up. They are meteors, or shooting stars. Bigger lumps that crash to Earth are meteorites. Comets are made of ice, frozen gases, and dust.

▷ Asteroids are also called the minor planets. Ceres, one of the largest asteroids, is about half as big as Pluto.

▽ This crater in Arizona was caused by a meteorite.

▷ As a comet
nears the sun, a
long tail streaks out
behind it. The tail
always points away
from the sun.

Facts About the Planets

- The Earth is the only planet in our solar system that is known to support life.

- Pluto was discovered by scientific detective work. Astronomers could not explain the orbits of Uranus and Neptune. It seemed as though the gravity of another planet was pulling on them. The astronomers worked out where they thought the ninth planet should be. When they studied the sky, they found Pluto.

- There may be a tenth planet beyond Pluto, waiting to be discovered.

Glossary

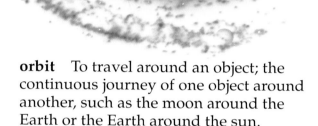

atmosphere The layer of gases that surrounds some planets. On Earth it allows us to breathe.

axis An imaginary line that runs through the center of a planet, around which the planet spins.

crater A bowl-shaped hole.

gravity An invisible force pulling objects together.

inner planets The planets between the Sun and the asteroid belt — Mercury, Venus, Earth, and Mars.

mass How much there is of something. An object's weight is affected by gravity; its mass is always the same.

moon A ball of rock or ice that orbits a planet.

orbit To travel around an object; the continuous journey of one object around another, such as the moon around the Earth or the Earth around the sun.

outer planets The planets beyond the asteroid belt — Jupiter, Saturn, Uranus, Neptune, and Pluto.

satellite Something that orbits a planet.

Index

Photographic credits: Bruce Coleman Ltd 13;
European Space Agency 3; Robert Harding Picture
Library 7; Hutchinson Library (Jeremy Horner) 15;
Dennis Milon/Space Photo Library 29; NASA 11, 16,
21, 23; NASA/Science Photo Library 18, 27;
NOAO/Science Photo Library 8; TRH Pictures 24.